iPhone 15 Pro Max User Guide for Seniors

Comprehensive Missing User Manual on How to Master the Device including New iOS Tips and Tricks

Michael L. Alston

iPhone 15 Pro Max Phone Guide

Table of Contents

Introduction to the iPhone 15 Pro Max

The iPhone 15 Pro Max is Apple's newest flagship smartphone, signifying the peak of innovation and technology in the world of mobile devices. Building upon the success of its predecessors, this exceptional phone provides a stunning mix of power, performance, and cutting-edge features.

Key Features & Highlights:

Brilliant Design: The iPhone 15 Pro Max sports a sleek and luxurious design with a ceramic back panel, reinforced frame, and a brilliant Super Retina XDR display that produces bright colors and deep blacks.

Pro-Level Photography: Equipped with a state-of-the-art camera system, this phone is a photographer's dream. Its powerful optics, computational photography, and night mode capabilities change mobile photography.

A15 Bionic Processor: Under the hood, the A15 Bionic processor drives the iPhone 15 Pro Max, bringing unrivaled speed and efficiency. Whether you're gaming, multitasking, or just surfing, this phone provides great performance.

5G Connection: Experience blazing-fast download and upload speeds with 5G connection, providing smooth streaming, online gaming, and video conferencing.

iOS Ecosystem: This iPhone easily connects with Apple's ecosystem, giving a single experience across all your Apple devices. It operates on the newest version of iOS, giving access to the latest features and upgrades.

Privacy and Security: Apple takes privacy seriously, and the iPhone 15 Pro Max is no exception. With features like Face ID and increased data security, your personal information stays safe.

Long Battery Life: Enjoy all-day battery life, even with intensive use. The iPhone 15 Pro Max is intended to keep up with your hectic lifestyle.

Before digging into the plethora of features and possibilities, it's vital to start with the fundamentals. In the following sections, we'll help you through the first setup, covering how to unbox your new iPhone, adjust basic settings, and become familiar with the user interface.

Whether you're a long-time Apple lover or a beginner to the iOS environment, this user guide will be your go-to resource for getting the most of your iPhone 15 Pro Max. We'll examine every part of this incredible technology, from making calls and capturing images to personalizing your smartphone to fit your needs.

Overview of Features

The iPhone 15 Pro Max is a powerhouse of technical innovation, packed with a broad variety of capabilities that raise your smartphone experience to new heights. In this part, we'll present an outline of its essential features:

Super Retina XDR Display: The iPhone 15 Pro Max sports a gorgeous Super Retina XDR display, giving vibrant colors, deep blacks, and high brightness levels. Whether you're viewing movies, playing games, or just surfing, the display gives an immersive visual experience.

A15 Bionic Processor: At the core of the iPhone 15 Pro Max lies the A15 Bionic processor, a powerhouse of computing power and efficiency. It offers seamless performance for all your activities, from gaming to multitasking.

Advanced Camera System: This phone boasts a cutting-edge camera system with various lenses, including ultra-wide, wide, and telephoto. It adds additional photographic features, including ProRAW and ProRes video recording, enabling you to take and edit professional-quality photographs and films.

5G Connectivity: With 5G capability, the iPhone 15 Pro Max provides lightning-fast download and upload rates, allowing smooth streaming, video conferencing, and online gaming. It also enables Dual SIM with eSIM for increased flexibility in mobile plans.

Face ID: Face ID, Apple's face recognition technology, offers a safe and simple method to unlock your phone, make secure payments, and authenticate applications and services.

iOS Ecosystem Integration: Seamlessly link your iPhone 15 Pro Max with your other Apple devices, such as Macs, iPads, and Apple Watch. This connection guarantees a consistent experience and seamless sharing of material.

Privacy and Security: Apple values your privacy and data security. Features like App Tracking Transparency and on-device Siri processing offer you control over your personal information.

MagSafe: The iPhone 15 Pro Max supports MagSafe accessories, allowing quick connection of magnetic cases, wallets, and wireless chargers for increased convenience.

All-Day Battery Life: Enjoy prolonged battery life, enabling you to use your phone throughout the day without stress. The phone also supports rapid charging and wireless charging.

Water and Dust Resistance: With an IP68 classification, the iPhone 15 Pro Max can endure submersion in water and is resistant to dust, making it robust for varied conditions.

Enhanced Augmented Reality (AR): AR capabilities are upgraded, allowing immersive AR experiences and applications that mix the digital and real worlds.

Sustainable Design: Apple continues to emphasize environmental responsibility with the use of recyclable materials and decreased carbon footprint in the production process.

These are just the highlights of what the iPhone 15 Pro Max has to offer. In the next parts of this user guide, we'll go further into each feature, equipping you with the knowledge and skills to make the most of your gadget. Whether you're a tech fanatic or a casual user, you'll learn how this smartphone may benefit your everyday life.

Getting Started

Unboxing Your iPhone: Carefully open the package and take the iPhone 15 Pro Max. Check the package for additional included components like the charger, EarPods, and a USB-C to Lightning cable.

Powering On Your iPhone: Press and hold the Side button (found on the right side of the device) until the Apple logo displays on the screen. This means that your iPhone is starting up.

Initial Setup: Choose your favorite language and location. Connect to Wi-Fi by choosing your network and inputting the password. Set up Face ID or Touch ID for security and authentication. Follow the on-screen prompts to register your face or fingerprint. Create or sign in using your Apple ID. This is needed for accessing the App Store, iCloud, and other Apple services.

Restore from Backup (Optional): If you're upgrading from a prior iPhone, you may opt to restore your data from an iCloud or iTunes backup during the setup process. This guarantees that your contacts, applications, images, and other data are moved to your new cell phone.

Set Up as new iPhone (Optional): If you wish to start fresh or if this is your first iPhone, you may pick "Set Up as New iPhone" to begin with a clean slate.

Modify Settings: Follow the on-screen prompts to modify settings like Siri, app analytics, and screen time preferences. You may always modify these options later in the options app.

Update iOS: After finishing the setup, check for any available iOS updates in the Settings app. Keeping your smartphone up to date guarantees you get the newest features and security fixes.

Explore the Home Screen: The Home Screen is where you'll locate your applications. Swipe left or right to travel between the displays, then press an app to launch it. The Dock, positioned at the bottom of the screen, enables easy access to commonly used programs.

Gesture Navigation: Familiarize yourself with gesture-based navigation, since the iPhone 15 Pro Max doesn't have a traditional Home button. Swipe up from the bottom to get to the Home Screen, swipe down from the top-right corner for the Control Center, and swipe from the sides to switch between applications.

App Store: Visit the App Store to download and install programs that you require. Use your Apple ID to make purchases.

iCloud and Data Sync: Set up iCloud to save your images, documents, and more on the cloud. This guarantees your info is available on all your Apple devices.

Enjoy Your New iPhone: Your iPhone 15 Pro Max is fully set up and ready for use! Explore its features, snap photographs, make calls, and modify it to fit your interests.

iPhone 15 Pro Max Phone Guide

This first setup is only the beginning of your iPhone 15 Pro Max experience. In the next parts of this book, we'll go further into numerous features and functions, helping you make the most of your new smartphone.

Configuring Wi-Fi and Cellular

Once you've switched up your iPhone 15 Pro Max and done the basic setup, the next critical step is to establish Wi-Fi and cellular connection. These settings are necessary for accessing the internet, making calls, and utilizing data-dependent applications. Here's how to set up Wi-Fi and cellular connections:

Connecting to Wi-Fi:

Access Wi-Fi Settings: Open the "Settings" app from your Home Screen. It looks like a gear symbol.

Wi-Fi Settings: In the "Settings" menu, touch on "Wi-Fi."

Turn on Wi-Fi: Toggle the button at the top of the screen to turn on Wi-Fi if it's not already enabled.

Select a Wi-Fi Network: Your iPhone will show a list of available Wi-Fi networks. Tap on your preferred network.

Enter Wi-Fi Password: If the network is protected, you'll be requested to enter the Wi-Fi password. Type it in and hit "Join."

Connected: Once properly connected, your iPhone will show a checkmark next to the Wi-Fi network's name.

Connecting to Cellular Data:

Check Cellular Signal: Ensure you have a cellular signal by checking the signal strength bars or the cellular symbol at the top of your screen. If you have a SIM card, it should be inserted and activated.

Enable Cellular Data: To utilize cellular data, make sure it's enabled. Go to "Settings" > "Cellular" and turn on "Cellular Data."

Data Roaming (Optional): If you're going overseas and want to utilize data, you may need to activate "Data Roaming" under the Cellular settings. Be warned that this may entail extra costs from your carrier.

Carrier Settings Update (Optional): Occasionally, your carrier may provide updates. If asked, touch "Update" to apply these updates.

Additional Cellular Settings (Optional): You may further adjust your cellular settings, such as allowing or blocking certain app access to cellular data, controlling your data use, and setting up personal hotspot.

By enabling Wi-Fi and cellular data, you guarantee that your iPhone 15 Pro Max can access the internet and remain connected whether you're at home, at work, or on the move. This connection is vital for software updates, online surfing, email, texting, and more.

Your Apple ID is your key to the Apple ecosystem, including iCloud, the App Store, and more. Setting up your Apple ID and iCloud account on your iPhone 15 Pro Max is necessary to use Apple's services and save your data safely in the cloud. Here's how to do it:

Creating or Signing In using an Apple ID:

Open Settings: Tap the "Settings" app on your iPhone. It's the gear-shaped symbol on your Home Screen.

Sign in to Your Apple ID: If you already have an Apple ID, touch "Sign in to your iPhone" at the top of the screen, and enter your Apple ID and password. Skip to step 5.

Create an Apple ID: If you don't have an Apple ID, press "Don't have an Apple ID or forget it?" then tap "Create Apple ID." Follow the on-screen directions to set up your new Apple ID, including entering your name, email address, and establishing a password.

Verification: You'll need to validate your identity by a verification code given to your email or a text message to your phone number. Follow the directions to finish this step.

Set Up iCloud: After logging in or establishing an Apple ID, you'll be requested to set up iCloud. iCloud is Apple's cloud storage and syncing service. Choose the data you wish to save in iCloud, including as Photos, Contacts, Calendars, and more. If you wish to utilize iCloud for backups, make sure "iCloud Backup" is set on. This will automatically backup your smartphone to iCloud while it's connected to Wi-Fi and charging.

iCloud Keychain (Optional): You may activate iCloud Keychain, which securely saves and syncs your passwords and payment information across your Apple devices.

Find My (Optional): Consider turning on "Find My iPhone" to find your smartphone if it's lost or stolen.

Complete Setup: Once you've chosen your preferences, press "Merge" or "Don't Merge" to mix your current device data with iCloud data, depending on your scenario. Read and agree to the Terms and Conditions.

Two-Factor Authentication (Recommended): For enhanced security, activate two-factor authentication for your Apple ID. This offers an extra layer of protection for your account.

With your Apple ID and iCloud set up, the iPhone 15 Pro Max will automatically sync your data across all your Apple devices, allow access to the App Store, and activate services like iCloud Backup and Find My iPhone. You may access and modify your iCloud settings at any time by heading to "Settings" > [your name] > "iCloud."

Navigating the Interface

The iPhone 15 Pro Max boasts a user-friendly UI with easy gestures and controls. Learning how to navigate the UI effectively is vital for getting the most of your gadget. Here's a tutorial to help you explore the interface:

Unlock Your iPhone: To unlock your iPhone, use Face ID (facial recognition) by staring at the screen, or if you have set up Touch ID, press your registered finger on the Home button. If neither is enabled, swipe up from the bottom of the screen and enter your passcode.

Home Screen: The Home Screen is where you'll locate your app icons and widgets. Swipe up from the bottom border or press the home indication at the bottom center to return to the Home Screen at any moment.

App Switcher: To switch between previously used applications, slide up from the bottom of the screen and pause momentarily. This launches the App Switcher, where you may swipe left or right to see and pick applications. Swipe up to dismiss an app.

Control Center: Access the Control Center by swiping down from the top-right corner of the screen (if you have a notch) or swiping up from the bottom edge (if you don't have a notch). Here, you may alter settings including Wi-Fi, brightness, and music playing.

Notifications: Swipe down from the top edge (or top-left corner if you have a notch) to display notifications. Swipe left on a notice to control it (e.g., clear, respond, or explore additional choices).

Siri: Activate Siri by saying, "Hey Siri," or pushing and holding the side button. You may ask Siri questions, create reminders, and operate numerous features with voice commands.

App Library: Swipe left on the Home Screen to enter the App Library, where your applications are arranged into categories. You may search for applications or press on a category to locate particular apps.

Search: To search for applications, contacts, or information on your smartphone, slide down from the center of the Home Screen or swipe right from the Home Screen.

Spotlight Search: Access Spotlight Search by sliding down on the Home Screen. It lets you search for applications, contacts, documents, and even online content.

Gestures: Use gestures for navigating. Swipe up from the bottom to return to the Home Screen, swipe down from the top-right for the Control Center, and swipe between applications by swiping from the sides.

Dock: The Dock, placed at the bottom of the Home Screen, enables fast access to your favorite and recently used applications. You may edit it to add your chosen applications.

Program Folders: You may arrange your applications into folders by dragging one program onto another. This is handy for keeping your Home Screen clutter-free.

AssistiveTouch (Optional): If you prefer on-screen navigation movements, you may activate AssistiveTouch under the Accessibility options.

These navigation techniques can help you effectively navigate about your iPhone 15 Pro Max's interface, making it simpler to access applications, settings, and alerts. Explore these gestures and controls to simplify your everyday interactions with your smartphone.

Home Screen Basics

The Home Screen is the center hub of your iPhone 15 Pro Max, where you can access your applications and widgets. Understanding the Home Screen and how to manage it may substantially increase your entire iPhone experience. Here are some essential components of the Home Screen:

App Icons: App icons are shortcuts to your installed programs. You may touch on an icon to access the related app.

App Folders: You may arrange app icons into folders to keep your Home Screen neat. To create a folder, drag one program icon onto another. You may also give the folder a custom name.

Dock: The Dock is a row of app icons at the bottom of the Home Screen. It stays displayed on all Home Screen pages and enables fast access to your most-used applications. You may personalize the Dock by adding or deleting program icons.

Widget Stack (Optional): iOS enables you to add widgets to your Home Screen for at-a-glance information. You can construct widget stacks by sliding widgets on top of each other. Swipe up or down on the stack to access various widgets.

Swiping Between Home Screen Pages: You may have many Home Screen pages to suit all your applications. Swipe left or right to move between these pages.

App Library: Swipe left on the Home Screen to open the App Library. This function automatically categorizes your programs, making it easier to discover and start them. You may also search for applications inside the App Library.

App Search: To quickly find an app on your Home Screen, slide down on the Home Screen (or swipe right from the main Home Screen) to see the Search bar. Start entering the app's name to locate it.

Rearrange and Delete Apps: To rearrange app icons, press and hold an app until they start jiggling. Then, drag an app to your preferred place or onto another app to form a folder. To remove an app, hit the "X" symbol in its top-left corner.

Customization: You may customize your Home Screen by changing the background. Go to "Settings" > "Wallpaper," and pick from Apple's wallpapers or your own photographs. You can also alter the look of your app icons with widgets from the App Store or third-party applications.

Home Screen Settings: In the "Settings" app, you may alter Home Screen settings, such as activating or disabling the App Library, adjusting the amount of app icons per row, and more.

Understanding the Home Screen and how to arrange it to your preference is crucial to effective navigation on your iPhone 15 Pro Max. You may organize your applications and widgets to fit your tastes and make it quick to access the programs you use most often.

Control Center and Notifications

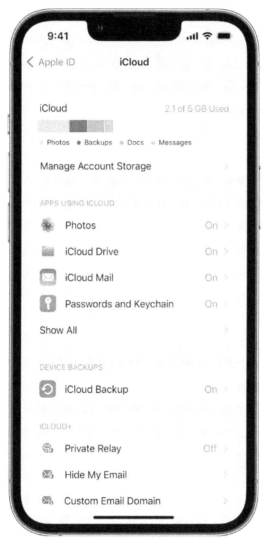

The Control Center and Notifications are crucial features on your iPhone 15 Pro Max that allow fast access to critical settings and enable you to remain informed on events, messages, and more. Here's how to utilize them effectively:

Control Center:

Access the Control Center: Swipe down from the top-right corner of the screen (or swipe up from the bottom of the screen, depending on your iOS version) to access the Control Center. It includes numerous toggles and shortcuts.

Control Center Components: The Control Center is separated into parts. You'll find buttons for Wi-Fi, Bluetooth, Do Not Disturb, and more in the top-left corner. The top-right area provides options like screen brightness and audio control. Below it, you have shortcuts for crucial tasks like the flashlight, camera, and calculator.

Customization: You may modify the Control Center by heading to "Settings" > "Control Center." Here, you can add or delete controls to adapt it to your tastes.

Access more Controls: To access more controls, including music playing, HomeKit devices, and more, slide down or up (depending on your iOS version) on the Control Center screen.

Control Center on the Lock Screen: You may reach the Control Center from the lock screen by swiping down (or up) from the top-right corner. However, certain functions may need verification if your smartphone is locked.

Notifications:

View Notifications: Notifications display on your lock screen and in the Notification Center, accessible by sliding down from the top of the screen. You may also read notifications immediately on the Home Screen if they are not hidden.

Interact with Notifications: Tap a notification to launch the related app or take action. For example, you may respond to a message or remove a reminder right from the notice.

Grouped Notifications: Notifications from the same app or discussion may be grouped together for easier management. You may enlarge or dissolve these groups as required.

Clearing Notifications: To remove individual notifications, slide them to the left or right and hit "remove." To delete all notifications, select "delete All."

Notification Settings: Customize how notifications behave by navigating to "Settings" > "Notifications." Here, you can change notification choices for each app, including noises, alerts, and badges.

Do Not Disturb: Use the Do Not Disturb function to stop alerts momentarily. You may schedule it, set it manually, or activate it while your device is locked.

These tools make it easier to change settings and keep informed on your iPhone 15 Pro Max. The Control Center enables easy access to critical tasks, while Notifications keep you up-to-date with messages and alerts from your applications. Customizing these features enables you to adapt your device to your individual requirements and interests.

Using Siri

Siri is your intelligent virtual assistant on the iPhone 15 Pro Max, capable of executing a broad variety of tasks via voice requests. Here's how to utilize Siri effectively:

Activate Siri:

Voice Activation: Say "Hey Siri" to activate Siri hands-free if this functionality is enabled in your settings. You may even use it when your iPhone is locked.

Manual Activation: If voice activation is switched off, press and hold the side button (found on the right side of your device) or the Home button (if you have one) until Siri shows on the screen.

Voice orders: You may ask Siri numerous questions and offer it orders, such as:

"What's the weather like today?"
"Set a timer for 10 minutes."
"Send a message to [contact's name]."
"Call [contact's name]."

"Play [song/artist/album] on Apple Music."

"Open [app name]."

"Remind me to [task] at [hour]."

Follow-Up Questions: Siri is context-aware, which means you may ask follow-up questions without repeating the context. For example, you may question, "Who is the President of the United States?" and then follow up with "How tall is he?" without stating "President of the United States" again.

Conversational Siri: You can have more natural conversations with Siri. For example, you may ask, "What movies are playing nearby?" and then follow up with, "What time is the next showing?"

Hands-Free Commands: While driving or while your hands are busy, Siri can execute operations like sending messages, making calls, and playing music without needing you to touch your smartphone.

Home Control: If you have smart home gadgets compatible with Apple's HomeKit, you can control them using Siri. For example, you may say, "Turn off the lights" or "Set the temperature to 72 degrees."

Dictation: You may use Siri for dictation. In any app that allows text input, enable Siri and say what you want to type. Siri will transcribe your voice into text.

Language and Accent Support: Siri supports numerous languages and accents. You may alter your Siri language and accent options in the Settings app.

Privacy: Apple takes privacy seriously, and Siri's interactions are meant to remain private. Siri queries are performed on your device wherever feasible, and your voice recordings are not tied with your Apple ID.

Siri Shortcuts (Optional): You may build Siri Shortcuts to automate various actions. For instance, you may establish a shortcut to send a predetermined message to a contact with a single Siri query.

Siri is a flexible tool that may simplify numerous chores and make your iPhone experience more efficient. Experiment with various voice commands and explore its possibilities to see how Siri can aid you in your everyday life.

Making Calls, Receiving Calls, Messages and Sending Text Messages

Your iPhone 15 Pro Max makes it simple to interact with friends and family via calls and text messages. Here's how to make and receive calls, send text messages, and utilize iMessage:

Making Calls:

Dialing a Number:

Open the Phone app from your Home Screen.

Tap the "Keypad" tab.

Enter the phone number you wish to call using the on-screen keyboard.

Tap the green call button to begin the call.

Using Contacts:

Open the Phone app.

Tap the "Contacts" option to access your stored contacts.

Select a contact and touch their phone number to make a call.

Voice Commands (Siri): Activate Siri by saying "Hey Siri" or holding the side button, then say "Call [contact's name]" or "Dial [phone number]."

Receiving Calls:

Answering Calls: When you get an incoming call, you can:

Tap the green answer button to answer the call.

Swipe up on the green phone icon to answer.

If you have a linked Bluetooth headset or AirPods, you may answer the call using them.

Declining Calls: To refuse a call, hit the red decline button, or press the side button (or top button, if you have one) twice.

Custom Responses (Optional): You may send a brief response to the caller while refusing a call. Tap "Message" and choose a pre-written answer or write a fresh one.

Sending Text Messages (SMS):

Using the Messages App:

Open the Messages app from your Home Screen.

Tap the compose button (typically a pencil or a new message symbol).

Enter the recipient's name or phone number in the "To:" area.

Type your message in the text area at the bottom.

Tap the blue send button to send the message.

Using iMessage (for Messages to Other Apple Devices):

Enable iMessage: To use iMessage, verify it's enabled in your device settings. Go to "Settings" > "Messages" and switch on "iMessage."

Sending iMessages:

Open the Messages app.

Compose a message like you would for an SMS, but send it to someone with an Apple device (i.e., another iPhone, iPad, or Mac).

iMessages display in blue bubbles, suggesting that they are transmitted via the internet instead of conventional SMS.

iMessage Features: iMessage includes features like read receipts (to check when your message is read), typing indications, the ability to transmit multimedia (pictures, videos, stickers, etc.), and more.

Group Messages: You may establish group iMessages to talk with numerous contacts concurrently.

These lessons cover the fundamentals of making and receiving calls, sending SMS text messages, and utilizing iMessage for richer text and multimedia communication. Feel free to explore additional sophisticated capabilities in the Phone and Messages applications to improve your communication experience on your iPhone 15 Pro Max.

FaceTime And iMessage

FaceTime and iMessage are two strong communication technologies that enable you to conduct video and audio conversations and exchange messages with other Apple users. Here's how to utilize FaceTime and iMessage effectively:

FaceTime:

Making FaceTime Calls:

Video Call: Open the FaceTime app from your Home Screen.

Tap the addition (+) icon at the upper right to start a new call.

Enter the contact's name, email, or phone number, and press their entry when it displays.
Tap the video camera icon to begin a video call.

Audio Call: Follow the same steps as above, but hit the phone symbol instead to begin an audio-only call.

Receiving FaceTime Calls: When someone begins a FaceTime call to you, you'll receive a notice. You may accept or refuse the call, or opt to send a message or set a reminder to call back.

FaceTime Features: During a FaceTime conversation, you may switch between the front and back cameras, mute your microphone, and change call volume. You may also apply filters and effects to improve your video.

FaceTime Group Calls (Optional): You may create group FaceTime calls by adding numerous contacts to the call. Just hit the Add (+) button and choose more participants.

iMessage:

Sending iMessages (Text and Multimedia Messages):

Open the Messages app from your Home Screen.

Compose a message by hitting the compose button.

Enter the recipient's name or phone number in the "To:" area.

Type your message in the text area at the bottom.

Tap the blue send button to send the message.

iMessage Features:

iMessage has various features:

Read Receipts: See when your message is read.

Typing Indicators: Know when the other person is typing a reply.

Multimedia Messages: Send photographs, movies, stickers, GIFs, and more.

Animoji and Emoji: Create animated characters and send messages with them.

Digital Touch: Send paintings, doodles, or your pulse.

Tap back: React to communications using emoticons (e.g., thumbs up, heart).

Group iMessages: You may establish group iMessages to talk with numerous contacts at once. Just create a new message and add numerous recipients.

iMessage applications & App Store: The Messages app includes its own App Store where you can download applications, stickers, games, and more to use inside your chats.

iMessage Settings: You may edit iMessage settings by navigating to "Settings" > "Messages." Here, you can activate or disable iMessage, alter message alerts, and more.

FaceTime and iMessage are easy methods to remain in contact with friends and family who use Apple products. You can make both audio and video calls using FaceTime and enjoy extensive texting options with iMessage, making conversation exciting and personal.

Managing Contacts

Keeping your contacts organized is vital for productive communication on your iPhone 15 Pro Max. Here's how to manage and keep your contacts effectively:

Adding Contacts:

From Phone App: Open the Phone app, hit the "Contacts" tab, and then press the plus (+) button to add a new contact. Enter the contact's data, such as name, phone number, email, and more.

From Contacts App: Open the Contacts app (often termed "Contacts" or "People"), hit the plus (+) button, and fill in the contact information.

Editing Contacts: To edit a contact, launch the Contacts app or access the contact from the Phone app, press the contact's name, and then select "Edit." Make the required changes and hit "Done" to save.

Deleting Contacts: To remove a contact, launch the Contacts app or access the contact from the Phone app, select "Edit," scroll down, and tap "remove Contact." Confirm the deletion.

Merging Duplicate Contacts: If you have duplicate contacts, you may combine them to keep your list clean. Open the Contacts app, pick a duplicate contact, press "Edit," scroll down, and tap "Link Contacts." Then, choose the contact to merge with.

Organizing Contacts into Groups: You may establish groups to classify your contacts. Open the Contacts app, touch "Groups" in the upper-left corner, and create new groups or add contacts to existing ones.

Backing Up Contacts: Your contacts are automatically backed up to iCloud if you have iCloud enabled. To check, go to "Settings" > [your name] > "iCloud" and make sure "Contacts" is switched on. This guarantees your contacts remain recoverable if you move to a different smartphone.

Exporting Contacts: You may export your contacts as a vCard or CSV file for backup or sharing. Go to the Contacts app, touch the contact you wish to export, hit "Share Contact," and pick the export format.

Importing Contacts: If you have contacts stored on your computer or in another format, you may import them to your iPhone. Go to the Contacts app, choose "Groups" > "All Contacts," then hit the plus (+) icon and select "Import."

Contact Syncing: Ensure your contacts sync across your devices. If you utilize iCloud, this should happen automatically. To verify, go to "Settings" > [your name] > "iCloud" and confirm "Contacts" is enabled.

Third-Party Contact Management applications: There are third-party applications available on the App Store that may help you manage and organize your contacts more effectively, giving capabilities like contact deduplication, backup, and more.

Keeping your contacts well-organized makes it simpler to discover and interact with the individuals that matter most. Whether you need to make calls, send messages, or set up FaceTime calls, having your contacts in order provides a pleasant experience on your iPhone 15 Pro Max.

Adding, Editing Contacts and Syncing Contacts

Adding Contacts:

From the Phone App:

Open the Phone app from your Home Screen.

Tap the "Contacts" tab at the bottom.

Tap the plus (+) icon in the upper-right corner.

Enter the contact's information, such as name, phone number, email, and more.

Tap "Done" to save the contact.

From the Contacts App:

Open the Contacts app from your Home Screen.

Tap the plus (+) icon in the upper-right corner.

Fill in the contact information.

Tap "Done" to save the contact.

Editing Contacts:

From the Contacts App:

Open the Contacts app.

Find and touch the contact you wish to modify.

Tap "Edit" in the top-right corner.

Modify the contact's details.

Tap "Done" to save the changes.

From the Phone App:

Open the Phone app.

Tap the "Contacts" tab.

Find and touch the contact you wish to modify.

Tap "Edit" in the top-right corner.

Update the contact's information.

Tap "Done" to save your changes.

Syncing Contacts:

iCloud Contacts Sync: Your iPhone may sync contacts with iCloud, Apple's cloud storage service. This guarantees that your contacts are backed up and accessible on all your Apple devices.

To enable iCloud Contacts sync:

Go to "Settings" > [your name] > "iCloud."

Make sure "Contacts" is switched on.

Your contacts will now sync with iCloud, and any changes you make will be mirrored across your Apple devices.

Google Contacts Sync:

If you use a Google account for contacts, you may sync them with your iPhone:

Go to "Settings" > "Passwords & Accounts."

Tap "Add Account," pick "Google," and sign in with your Google account.

Turn on "Contacts."

Your Google contacts will now sync with your iPhone.

Microsoft Exchange Contacts Sync:

If you use Microsoft Exchange for contacts, you may set up your account to sync with your iPhone:

Go to "Settings" > "Passwords & Accounts."

Tap "Add Account," pick "Microsoft Exchange," and input your Exchange account information.

Turn on "Contacts."

Your Exchange contacts will now sync with your iPhone.

Other Accounts: Many other email services and applications provide contact synchronization possibilities. You may set up these accounts in the "Passwords & Accounts" section of your iPhone's settings to sync their contacts.

By adding, modifying, and synchronizing your contacts, you guarantee that your address book is up to date and available across all your devices, making it simpler to interact with your contacts on your iPhone 15 Pro Max.

Camera and Photography

Your iPhone 15 Pro Max includes a strong camera system that enables you to create great images and movies. Here are some suggestions to make the most of your camera and enhance your photography skills:

Understanding Camera Modes: Your iPhone has different camera modes, including Photo, Video, Portrait, Night, and more. Swipe left or right on the camera interface to move between different modes. Experiment with various settings to complement the situation.

HDR (High Dynamic Range): HDR setting helps capture higher information in high-contrast images. It blends numerous exposures into one picture. Turn on "Auto HDR" in the camera settings to allow the iPhone determine when to utilize it, or manually activate HDR as required.

Composition: Apply fundamental photographic concepts like the rule of thirds. Use gridlines (accessible in camera options) to assist align your subjects. Experiment with various angles and perspectives for unique photos.

Focus and Exposure: Tap on your screen to set the focus and exposure point. You may adjust exposure by swiping up or down after tapping.

Portrait Mode: Use Portrait mode to make professional-looking images with a blurred backdrop (bokeh effect). This method works for both human and non-human beings.

Night Mode: In low-light circumstances, Night mode automatically activates to take well-exposed and detailed photographs. Keep your smartphone stable when shooting Night mode photographs for the best effects.

ProRAW and ProRes Video (Optional): If you're interested in sophisticated photography or video, consider utilizing ProRAW for images and ProRes for video. These formats allow additional control over post-processing.

Editing Tools: Use the built-in editing tools in the Photos app to improve your photographs. You may edit exposure, color, cut, and add filters. Experiment with these tools to fine-tune your images.

Live Photos: Live Photos record a few seconds of video before and after capturing a snapshot. You may use them to create dynamic graphics or pick the best frame from the series.

Burst Mode: Hold down the shutter button to activate Burst mode, which snaps a sequence of shots fast. This is fantastic for catching fast-moving subjects or ensuring you capture the perfect photo in action settings.

Selfies & Front Camera: The front camera of your iPhone 15 Pro Max is capable of capturing high-quality selfies. Use Portrait mode, filters, and selfie editing tools for amazing self-portraits.

Storage and Backup: Since iPhone images and videos may take up substantial storage space, consider utilizing iCloud or other cloud storage services for backup. This way, you can clear up space on your smartphone while keeping your memories intact.

Accessories: Explore photography accessories like tripods, external lenses, and gimbals to further improve your iPhone photos.

Practice, explore, and learn from your images to enhance your photography talents with your iPhone 15 Pro Max. With its powerful camera functions and user-friendly design, you have the ability to capture breathtaking moments in any setting.

Using the Camera App

The Camera app on your iPhone 15 Pro Max is meant to be user-friendly while giving a broad variety of options for producing excellent images and movies. Here's how to utilize the Camera app effectively:

Opening the Camera App: From your Home Screen, hit the "Camera" icon to launch the Camera app instantly. You may also access the Camera from the Control Center by swiping down from the top-right corner (if enabled).

Basic Shooting Modes: When you start the Camera app, you're in the default "Photo" mode. Swipe left or right on the screen to switch between various shooting modes including Photo, Video, Portrait, and more.

Auto Focus and Exposure: Tap anywhere on the screen to adjust the focus and exposure point. You may also drag your finger up or down to manually adjust exposure.

Shutter Button: The huge circular button at the bottom of the screen is the shutter button. Tap it to snap a picture. For videos, touch it to start recording and press it again to stop.

Zoom: Pinch in or out on the screen to zoom in or out. On the iPhone 15 Pro Max, you have access to optical zoom, which gives exceptional picture quality even when zoomed in.

Live Photo: Enable Live Photo by clicking the symbol at the top of the screen (it looks like concentric circles). Live Photos record a few seconds of video before and after the snap, giving a dynamic touch to your images.

Flash: Adjust the flash setting by touching the lightning bolt symbol. Options include Auto, On, Off, and Slow Sync (helpful for low-light scenarios).

Timer: Tap the timer icon (looks like a clock) to set a timer for capturing images or movies. This might be helpful for group photographs or selfies.

Filters: Tap the three overlapping circles symbol to access different filters. Experiment with these to apply various effects to your images in real-time.

Portrait Mode: In Portrait mode, you can shoot professional-looking images with a blurred backdrop (bokeh). Swipe to Portrait mode and follow on-screen directions for ideal framing.

Night Mode: Night mode activates automatically in low-light settings. It helps you to shoot well-exposed and detailed photographs even in the dark. Ensure your smartphone is stable when capturing Night mode photographs.

Switching Cameras: To switch between the rear and front cameras, touch the camera swap symbol (two arrows in a circular motion). Use the front camera for selfies and video calls.

Picture Review: After snapping a picture, touch the thumbnail preview in the bottom-left corner to review it. Swipe left or right to explore more recent images.

Settings: Access camera settings by touching the arrow icon at the top or by heading to "Settings" > "Camera." Here, you may specify grid lines, formats, and more.

Quick open (Optional): On the lock screen, you may quickly open the Camera app by swiping left from the right side of the screen.

Feel free to explore and experiment with the Camera app's numerous modes and settings to unleash your creativity and shoot stunning images and films on your iPhone 15 Pro Max.

Photo and Video Capture

Your iPhone 15 Pro Max is equipped with a strong camera system capable of taking high-quality images and movies. Here's how to shoot images and record movies effectively:

Taking Photos:

Access the Camera App: ON your Home Screen, press the "Camera" icon to access the Camera app.

Focus and Exposure: Tap anywhere on the screen to set the focus and exposure point. The camera will change settings appropriately.

Shutter Button: The huge circular button at the bottom of the screen is the shutter button. Tap it to snap a picture.

Live Photos (Optional): If you wish to take a Live Photo (a brief video clip with audio before and after the photo), make sure the Live Photos icon (concentric circles) is activated at the top of the screen.

Zoom: Pinch in or out on the screen to zoom in or out. On the iPhone 15 Pro Max, you get optical zoom for exceptional picture quality when zooming.

HDR (High Dynamic Range): HDR setting helps capture higher information in high-contrast images. The iPhone may automatically activate it when required. Look for the "HDR" label at the top of the screen.

Flash (Optional): Adjust the flash setting by touching the lightning bolt symbol. Options include Auto, On, Off, and Slow Sync (helpful for low-light scenarios).

Timer (Optional): Set a timer for snapping images by touching the timer icon (which looks like a clock) at the top of the screen. This might be helpful for group photographs or selfies.

Portrait Mode (Optional): For images with a blurred backdrop (bokeh effect), swipe to Portrait mode and follow on-screen directions for ideal framing.

Night Mode (Optional): Night mode activates automatically in low-light settings. Ensure your smartphone is stable when shooting Night mode images for well-exposed photos.

Recording Videos:

Access the Camera App: On your Home Screen, press the "Camera" icon to access the Camera app.

Switch to Video Mode: Swipe to the "Video" mode by swiping left or pressing the word "Video" on the screen.

Start Recording: Tap the record button to start recording a video. The timer at the top will show you the length of your movie.

Zoom (Optional): You may zoom in or out while recording by pinching in or out on the screen. Remember that optical zoom delivers the greatest quality.

Alter Focus and Exposure (Optional): While recording, you may touch the screen to alter the focus and exposure point.

Stop Recording: To stop recording, press the record button again. The Photos app will have the video file.

Video Settings (Optional): You may modify video settings like resolution and frame rate by navigating to "Settings" > "Camera" > "Record Video."

Time-Lapse and Slow-Mo (Optional): The Camera app features modes like Time-Lapse and Slow-Mo for creative video shooting. Swipe to these modes and hit the record button to start recording.

Experiment with these tools to produce great images and movies on your iPhone 15 Pro Max. The more you practice, the better your photography and filmmaking talents will get.

Editing Photos and Videos

Your iPhone 15 Pro Max has a powerful range of tools for editing images and movies straight inside the images app. Here's how to improve your media:

Editing Photos:

Open the Photos App: Tap the "Photos" app icon on your Home Screen.

Select a picture: Find and tap on the picture you wish to modify to open it.

Edit Mode: Tap the "Edit" button at the top right of the screen to enter edit mode.

Basic Editing Tools: You'll notice numerous editing tools at the bottom of the screen:

Crop/Rotate: Use the crop tool to trim or rotate the picture.

Filters: Apply several filters for diverse effects.

Adjustments: Fine-tune brightness, exposure, contrast, and more.

Retouch: Remove defects or undesired things.

Markup: Add text, shapes, or your signature.

Filters: Apply different creative filters.

Live Photos: If you have a Live Photo, you may pick a new key photo or add effects like bounce or loop.

Undo and Redo: If you make a mistake, utilize the undo and redo buttons in the upper left of the screen.

Save Changes: Once you're pleased with your adjustments, hit "Done" to save the changed picture. The original picture is maintained, and the adjustments are stored as a second copy.

Revert to Original: If you wish to revert to the original picture at any point, press "Revert" while in edit mode.

Editing Videos:

Open the Photos App: Tap the "Photos" app icon on your Home Screen.

Select a Video: Find and tap on the video you want to modify to open it.

Edit Mode: All you have to do is click the "Edit" button at the bottom of the screen to get into edit mode.

Trimming Videos: To trim a video, drag the yellow handles at the beginning and end of the timeline to pick the appropriate part. Then, touch "Trim" to save the reduced video.

Video Filters: You may add video filters by touching the filters icon. Experiment with various filters to vary the appearance of your movie.

Adjust Video: Tap the "Adjust" icon to fine-tune parameters like exposure, brightness, contrast, and more for your video.

Rotate and Crop: The rotate and crop tools enable you to modify the orientation and frame of your video.

Speed: You may modify the speed of your video by touching the "Speed" symbol. Speed it up or slow it down for creative effects.

Undo and Redo: If you make a mistake, utilize the undo and redo buttons in the bottom left of the screen.

Save Changes: Once pleased with your video adjustments, hit "Done" to save the altered video. The original video is maintained, while the modifications are stored as a separate copy.

Return to Original: If you wish to return to the original video at any moment, press "Revert" while in edit mode.

Utilizing these editing features in the photographs app, you can improve your photographs and videos, remove blemishes, and add creative touches to your material directly on your iPhone 15 Pro Max. Experiment with various modifications and filters to reach the desired results.

Internet and Connectivity

Your iPhone 15 Pro Max provides many methods to connect to the internet and remain associated with others. Here's how to adjust your internet and connection settings:

Wi-Fi Connection:

To connect to a Wi-Fi network:

Go to "Settings" > "Wi-Fi."

Toggle the Wi-Fi switch on.

From the list, choose your Wi-Fi network, then enter the password if necessary.

Your iPhone will automatically connect to recognized Wi-Fi networks when available.

Cellular Data: Your iPhone utilizes cellular data while not connecting to Wi-Fi. To control cellular data:

Go to "Settings" > "Cellular."

Here, you may activate or stop cellular data, monitor data use, and manage app-specific cellular data settings.

Airplane Mode: Enabling Airplane Mode shuts off all wireless connectivity, including cellular, Wi-Fi, and Bluetooth. You may switch it on from the Control Center or in the Settings app.

Bluetooth: To connect Bluetooth devices (e.g., headphones, speakers, or a vehicle), go to "Settings" > "Bluetooth." Turn on Bluetooth, and your iPhone will look for nearby devices to pair with.

Personal Hotspot: You may use your iPhone as a personal hotspot to share its cellular data connection with other devices. Go to "Settings" > "Personal Hotspot" to set it up.

VPN (Virtual Private Network): If you make use of VPN for enhanced privacy and protection, you may set it under "Settings" > "VPN." Add your VPN profile to connect to a private network.

Cellular Data Roaming: When traveling overseas, be careful of data roaming rates. You may deactivate data roaming under "Settings" > "Cellular" > "Cellular Data Options."

5G Connection: The iPhone 15 Pro Max features a 5G connection for better internet speeds in locations with 5G coverage. You may set or turn off 5G under "Settings" > "Cellular" > "Cellular Data Options" > "Voice & Data."

Network and Wi-Fi Troubleshooting: If you're having connection troubles, you can:

Toggle Wi-Fi and cellular data off and on.

Restart your iPhone.

Reset network settings under "Settings" > "General" > "Reset" > "Reset Network Settings."

For more assistance, speak with your internet service provider or carrier.

Wi-Fi Calling and FaceTime Audio: You can make calls over Wi-Fi with Wi-Fi Calling and utilize FaceTime Audio for high-quality audio calls over the internet. Ensure these functionalities are enabled in your iPhone settings.

Mobile Hotspot and Tethering: You may share your iPhone's internet connection with other devices utilizing personal hotspot and tethering. Set up and customize these parameters under the "Personal Hotspot" section of the settings.

Automatic Wi-Fi Connection (Auto-Join): Your iPhone may automatically connect to recognized Wi-Fi networks. To activate or turn off this function, go to "Settings" > "Wi-Fi" > choose a network > turn "Auto-Join" on or off.

Managing your internet and connection settings can help you remain connected, maximize your iPhone 15 Pro Max's capabilities, and guarantee a seamless online experience.

Browsing using Safari

Safari is the pre-installed web browser on your iPhone 15 Pro Max, and it delivers a quick and user-friendly online surfing experience. Here's how to surf the web using Safari:

Open Safari: Tap the Safari icon on your Home Screen to activate the browser.

Address Bar: At the top of the screen, you'll find the address bar. Tap on it to input a web address (URL) or search for anything using a search engine like Google.

Tabs: To launch a new account, hit the square icon in the bottom-right corner. You may have numerous tabs open concurrently. Swipe left or right on the tabs bar at the bottom to move between them.

Navigation: Use the back arrow (<) and forward arrow (>) buttons in the bottom-left corner to browse across websites you've viewed.

Refresh and Stop: The circular arrow symbol in the address bar is the refresh button. Tap it to refresh the current page. If a website is loading and you wish to end it, hit the "X" symbol that displays next to the URL.

Sharing and Bookmarks: To share, bookmark, and add to your reading list, simply tap the share sign (a square with an arrow pointing up) at the bottom of the screen.

Reading List: You may store articles on your reading list to read later, even offline. To access your reading list, hit the book symbol at the bottom and pick the glasses icon.

Search ideas: As you enter the address bar, Safari will display search ideas and website recommendations depending on your input.

Private Browser: To surf privately, hit the tab switcher button in the bottom-right corner and then pick "Private." This disables Safari from keeping your browser history and cookies.

Reader View: For a distraction-free reading experience on supported websites, touch the reader view symbol in the URL bar (it looks like a book).

Downloads (Optional): Safari can download files. When you touch a download link, Safari will ask whether you wish to download the file. You may access your downloads by hitting the download symbol in the bottom-right corner.

Customization: Safari provides different options and preferences you may alter. Go to "Settings" > "Safari" to customize features, including search engine choice, pop-up blocking, and content blockers.

Tabs Grouping (Optional): You may group relevant tabs in Safari for greater organization. To accomplish this, press and hold on a tab, then choose "Move to Group."

Reader View (Optional): When available on a site, you may press the "Reader" symbol in the URL bar to transition to a simpler, more legible page version.

Quick Website Access: Safari can offer you quick website previews when you press and hold a link. This enables you to glance at a webpage without completely viewing it.

Safari on your iPhone 15 Pro Max delivers a smooth online surfing experience with features geared for efficiency and ease. Whether you're looking for information, reading articles, or browsing websites, Safari has you covered.

Connecting to Wi-Fi and Bluetooth and Using AirDrop

Connecting to Wi-Fi Bluetooth and utilizing AirDrop are important chores on your iPhone 15 Pro Max. Here's how to perform each of them:

Connecting to Wi-Fi:

Open Settings: From your Home Screen, select the "Settings" app.

Wi-Fi Settings: Tap "Wi-Fi" in the settings menu.

Turn On Wi-Fi: Toggle the button at the top to turn on Wi-Fi.

Select a Network: Under "Choose a Network," your iPhone will list available Wi-Fi networks. Tap on the network to which you want to join.

Enter Wi-Fi Password: If the network is password-protected, enter the Wi-Fi password when requested, and then touch "Join."

Connected: Once you see a checkmark next to the Wi-Fi network's name, you're connected.

Connecting to Bluetooth:

Open Settings: From your Home Screen, select the "Settings" app.

Bluetooth Settings: Tap "Bluetooth" in the settings menu.

Turn On Bluetooth: Toggle the button at the top to turn on Bluetooth.

Pairing Devices: Your iPhone will automatically look for nearby Bluetooth devices. When you see the device you wish to connect to, touch it to start the pairing procedure.

Follow on-screen Instructions: Depending on the device, you may need to enter a password or touch "Pair" on both smartphones. To complete the pairing, follow the on-screen instructions.

Connected: Once linked, your iPhone will remember the device, and it should connect instantly when in range.

Using AirDrop:

Enable Bluetooth and Wi-Fi: Ensure Bluetooth and Wi-Fi are switched on. You may accomplish this via the Control Center or the settings indicated above.

Open the File to Share: To transmit a file via AirDrop, open the file (e.g., a picture, video, or document) in the corresponding app (e.g., Photos, Files, etc.).

Tap the Share Button: Press the share button, like a square with an upward-pointing arrow.

Select AirDrop Recipient: Under the AirDrop section, you'll notice nearby AirDrop-enabled devices. To share the file with another device, tap on it.

Receiver Accepts: The receiver will get a notice and may choose to accept or deny the file. If they accept, the file will be transmitted.

Remember to use AirDrop properly, particularly when set to "Everyone" visibility. Make sure you're delivering files to the appropriate recipient.

Following these instructions, you may effortlessly connect to Wi-Fi and Bluetooth and utilize AirDrop for smooth file sharing on your iPhone 15 Pro Max.

Apps and App Store

Your iPhone 15 Pro Max has a choice of pre-installed applications, and you may download new apps from the App Store. Here's how to utilize and manage your apps:

Using Pre-installed Apps:

Home Screen: Your applications are shown on the Home Screen. Swipe left or right to access various screens and discover your applications.

App Folders: You may arrange applications by creating folders. To build a folder, press and hold an app icon until it wiggles, then drag it onto another app to form a folder.

Launching Apps: Tap on an app icon to launch it.

App Switcher: To switch between previously used applications, slide up from the bottom and stop in the center of the screen (or swipe up and to the right if you have a Home Button).

App Library: On your home screen, swipe right to access the app library, where applications are automatically organized.

Downloading Apps from the App Store:

App Store Icon: You may touch the "App Store" icon on your Home Screen.

Search for applications: Use the search box at the bottom to search for applications by name or category.

Browse and Download: Browse the App Store to find new applications or touch on a single app to explore its information. To download an app, hit "Get" or the app's pricing.

Face ID/Touch ID and Password: Authenticate your download using Face ID/Touch ID or by entering your Apple ID password.

Updates: App updates are crucial for security and performance. To update applications, visit the App Store, press your profile symbol in the upper right, then scroll down to view available updates.

App Offloading (Optional): If your smartphone is running short on capacity, you may activate "Offload Unused programs" under "Settings" > "App Store." This will remove programs you don't use regularly but save their data.

Deleting Apps:

Tap and Hold: Hold the app icon until it wiggles.

Delete Option: An "X" will show on specific program icons. Tap the "X" to uninstall the program. Be cautious; this will erase the app and its data.

Confirm Deletion: A confirmation notice will be displayed. Tap "Delete" to confirm.

Re-downloading Deleted Apps: If you mistakenly delete an app or wish to reload it:

Open the App Store.

In the upper right corner, tap the profile symbol.

Go to "Purchased."

Find the deleted app and touch the download symbol (cloud with an arrow).

App Permissions: Apps may seek access to different device functionalities, including location, camera, and microphone. You may adjust these permissions in "Settings" > "Privacy."

Managing your applications and browsing the App Store will enable you to tailor your iPhone 15 Pro Max to meet your requirements and hobbies, bringing usefulness and enjoyment to your smartphone.

Installing, Updating Apps and Organizing Apps

Here are step-by-step instructions on how to install, update, and manage applications on your iPhone 15 Pro Max:

Installing Apps:

Open the App Store: Tap the "App Store" icon on your Home Screen.

Search for an App: Use the search box at the bottom to locate the app you want. You may search by name, category, or keywords.

Select and Download: Tap the app you wish to install to see its information. Then, press the "Get" button (or the fee if it's a premium app).

Authenticate Download: To verify the download, use Face ID Touch ID or enter your Apple ID password when prompted.

Wait for Download: The app will begin downloading and installing on your device. You can check the progress on your Home Screen.

Updating Apps:

Open the App Store: Tap the "App Store" icon.

Go to Updates: At the bottom right, press the "Updates" tab. You'll see a list of available app updates.

Update All applications: To update all applications at once, touch "Update All" in the top right. Or, update individual applications by pressing "Update" next to each one.

Authenticate Update: If asked, use Face ID, Touch ID, or your Apple ID password to validate the upgrades.

Wait for Updates: The applications will start upgrading. You can follow the development on the Updates tab.

Organizing Apps:

Create Folders: To create a folder, press and hold an app icon until it wiggles. Then, drag one app onto another. This creates a folder. You may name it and add other applications to it.

Move applications: To move applications around or between folders, press and hold an app icon until it wiggles. Then, drag it to your chosen spot.

Delete applications: To delete applications, press and hold an app icon until it wiggles. Tap the "X" symbol on the app you wish to uninstall, then confirm. Be careful since this eliminates the app and its data.

App Library: On your home screen, swipe right to access the app library. It automatically categorizes your applications for quick access.

Search for applications: You may easily locate applications by sliding down on the Home Screen to show the search bar and inputting the app's name.

Conceal Home Screen Pages: You may conceal individual Home Screen pages to decrease clutter. Press and hold on to the Home Screen, press the dots at the bottom, then uncheck the sites you wish to hide.

By following these instructions, you can effectively install, update, and manage applications on your iPhone 15 Pro Max, guaranteeing a neat and customized app experience.

App Store Overview

The App Store is your entrance to a broad world of applications intended to improve your iPhone 15 Pro Max's capabilities and cater to your interests and requirements. Here's an introduction to how to explore and use the App Store:

Access the App Store: The App Store icon looks like a blue "A" on a white background. Tap this icon on your Home Screen to enter the App Store.

App Store Tabs: The App Store is arranged into various tabs at the bottom:

Today: Discover notable applications, articles, and app collections handpicked by the App Store team.

Games: Explore a range of games, from casual to deep, and access in-app purchases.

Applications: Find applications for many reasons, including productivity, entertainment, utility, and more.

Arcade: Access games accessible via Apple Arcade, a subscription-based gaming service.

Search: Search for particular applications or browse by category.

App information: When you touch on an app, you'll view its information page. Here, you can read the app's description, check user reviews and ratings, see images and videos, and get information on in-app purchases.

Get & Install Apps: To download an app, touch the "Get" button (or the fee if it's a paid app). Authenticate the download using Face ID, Touch ID, or your Apple ID password.

Updates: The "Updates" page provides updates for your installed applications. You may update applications individually or choose "Update All" to update them together.

Account and Profile: To access your account settings, including your Apple ID, payment details, and app subscriptions, tap the profile symbol in the top right corner.

Wish List: You may add applications to your Wish List to keep track of apps you're interested in. Just touch the heart symbol on the app's details page.

Search and Discover: Use the search box to locate particular applications or browse curated collections and charts to discover new and popular apps.

App Ratings and Reviews: Before downloading, check the app's user ratings and read reviews to judge its quality and dependability.

Family Sharing: If you enable Family Sharing, you may share your bought applications with family members. Each family member has their own Apple ID but may access shared applications without paying them individually.

App Store Settings: Customize your App Store experience by navigating to "Settings" > "App Store." Here, you may activate automatic app updates, allow or turn off in-app ratings and reviews, and establish permissions for app downloads over cellular connection.

Redeem Gift Cards and Promo Codes: You may redeem gift cards and promo codes for applications, in-app purchases, or Apple Store credit by touching your profile symbol and choosing "Redeem Gift Card or Code."

The App Store is a dynamic and continually expanding marketplace, providing a broad choice of programs to fit your requirements and interests. Explore, download, and enjoy the many applications to improve your iPhone 15 Pro Max experience.

Settings & Customization

Your iPhone 15 Pro Max includes many settings and customization choices to adapt your smartphone to your liking. Here's how to access and utilize these settings:

Accessing Settings: Open Settings: Tap the "Settings" app icon on your Home Screen. It looks like a gear.

Navigating Settings: Inside the Settings app, you'll discover many sections with distinct customization choices. Scroll down to explore these areas.

Common Settings and Customization Options:

Wi-Fi and Bluetooth: In "Settings," you may activate or disable Wi-Fi and Bluetooth, connect to networks and devices, and modify network and Bluetooth settings.

Display & Brightness: Adjust screen brightness, activate Dark Mode, select text size, and pick a background.

Noises & Haptics: Customize ringtones, notification noises, and vibration settings. Adjust volume and haptic feedback preferences.

Alerts: Manage notification settings for each app, enabling you to choose how and when you get alerts.

Privacy: Control app permissions for location, camera, microphone, and more. Manage data tracking and location services.

Control Center: Customize the Control Center to include your most-used functions and controls. You may add or delete Wi-Fi, Bluetooth, and screen recording.

Battery: Monitor battery consumption, select Low Power Mode, and see battery health—Configure battery-related parameters.

Do Not Disturb: Schedule "Do Not Disturb" intervals, activate sleep mode, and configure "Do Not Disturb While Driving."

Screen Time: Track your device use, establish app limitations, and plan "Downtime" for a digital detox.

Accessibility: Customize accessibility options, such as text-to-speech, display accommodations, and gesture controls.

Face ID/Touch ID & Passcode: Configure security settings, such as Face ID or Touch ID, and establish a passcode or password for device access.

General: Access device-wide settings, including language, region, keyboard, and reset choices.

Siri & Search: Customize Siri's behavior and speech options. Manage Siri recommendations and search options.

Software Update: Check for and apply software updates to keep your device safe and up-to-date.

App Store: Configure settings relating to app downloads, automated updates, and cellular data consumption for applications.

Privacy & Security: Manage privacy and security settings, including location services, app tracking, and content controls.

Family Sharing: Set up and manage Family Sharing for shared purchases and parental controls.

iTunes & App Store: Adjust settings for App Store downloads and updates, including cellular data use.

Home Screen: Customize Home Screen settings, such as app icon size and library structure.

Accessibility Shortcut: Set up accessibility shortcuts for easy access to various functions.

These are just a few examples of the various settings and customization choices available on your iPhone 15 Pro Max. Explore these options to make your smartphone perform how you want it to and improve your overall iPhone experience.

System Preferences & Personalizing Your iPhone

Customizing your iPhone 15 Pro Max enables you to customize it to your tastes and make it yours. Here are some system choices and customization options:

Wallpaper: To select a wallpaper for your home screen and lock screen, go to "Settings" > "Wallpaper" > "Choose a New Wallpaper."

Widgets: Swipe right on your Home Screen to enter the Today View, where you can add, delete, and edit widgets for fast access to information and app shortcuts.

App Icons: Some applications provide personalized app icons. To change an app's icon, go to "Settings" > "Display & Brightness" > "Home Screen Layout," then select "App Icon." Select the symbol you want.

Home Screen Organization: Organize your applications into folders or move them about your Home Screen to create a layout that meets your preferences.

Control Center: Customize the Control Center by heading to "Settings" > "Control Center." Here, you may add or delete controls and change their arrangement.

Noises & Haptics: Adjust ringtones, notification noises, and vibration patterns for calls, texts, and applications under "Settings" > "Sounds & Haptics."

Accessibility: Personalize your iPhone's accessibility options, including font size, display accommodations, and gesture controls, under "Options" > "Accessibility."

Do Not Disturb: Schedule "Do Not Disturb" intervals and adjust its behavior under "Settings" > "Do Not Disturb."

Siri: Customize Siri's voice, language, and behavior under "Settings" > "Siri & Search."

Face ID/Touch ID & Passcode: Configure your device's security settings, including Face ID/Touch ID and passcodes, under "Settings" > "Face ID & Passcode" or "Touch ID & Passcode."

Display & Brightness: Adjust display settings, such as brightness, text size, and dark mode, under "Settings" > "Display & Brightness."

Privacy & Security: Manage privacy settings, location services, app tracking, and content limitations in "Settings" > "Privacy & Security."

Language & Region: Change your device's language, region, and calendar settings under "Settings" > "Language & Region."

Family Sharing: Set up Family Sharing and share purchases with family members under "Settings" > "Family Sharing."

iTunes & App Store: Configure settings relating to app downloads, automatic updates, and cellular data consumption for applications under "Settings" > "iTunes & App Store."

Home Screen: Customize Home Screen settings, such as app icon size and app library structure, under "Settings" > "Home Screen."

Mail, Contacts, and Calendars: Personalize email signatures, sync accounts, and change calendar preferences in "Settings" > "Mail" and "Settings" > "Contacts" or "Settings" > "Calendar."

Background App update: Control which applications may update information in the background under "Settings" > "General" > "Background App Refresh."

App rights: Manage individual app rights, such as location and camera access, under "Settings" > "Privacy."

Safari Settings: Customize Safari's functionality, including privacy settings and content blockers, under "Settings" > "Safari."

By exploring these system settings and customization choices, you can make your iPhone 15 Pro Max perform and look precisely how you want it to, boosting your overall user experience.

Privacy and Security

Face ID/Touch ID and Passcode: You may set up Face ID (if available) or Touch ID for biometric authentication or use a passcode for device access. Go to "Settings" > "Face ID & Passcode" or "Touch ID & Passcode" to adjust these options.

App Permissions: Control which applications have access to your device's functions, including location, camera, microphone, and contacts, under "Settings" > "Privacy."

Location Services: Manage app-specific location access and check location history under "Settings" > "Privacy" > "Location Services." You may enable location access constantly, just while using the app, or never.

Safari Privacy Settings: Enhance your online privacy by activating tools like Intelligent Tracking Prevention and content filters under "Settings" > "Safari."

iCloud Security: Secure your iCloud account by using two-factor authentication. Go to "Settings" > [your name] > "Password & Security" > "Two-Factor Authentication."

App Store Privacy Labels: Check app privacy labels on the App Store to learn how applications gather and utilize your data before installing.

App Tracking Transparency: With App Tracking Transparency, you can Control which applications may follow your behavior across other apps and websites. You'll get prompts asking for permission when applications wish to monitor you. You may adjust this under "Settings" > "Privacy" > "Tracking."

Safari Privacy Report: In Safari, you may read a Privacy Report that details how websites monitor your browsing habits and what content blocks are active. Access this by pressing the "AA" symbol in the address bar and choosing "Privacy Report."

Password Management: Use the built-in iCloud Keychain or a third-party password manager to store and autofill passwords securely. You may adjust this under "Settings" > "Passwords & Accounts" > "AutoFill Passwords."

Find My iPhone: Enable Find My iPhone to find your handset if it's lost or stolen. You may customize this under "Settings" > [your name] > "Find My" > "Find My iPhone."

Data Encryption: Your iPhone encrypts data by default, making it impossible for unwanted access. Encryption safeguards your data, including messages, photographs, and files.

App Privacy Report: Review the App Privacy Report in "Settings" > "Privacy" to discover how frequently applications have accessed your data in the previous seven days.

Device Lock: Your device automatically locks after a period of inactivity. Configure the auto-lock time in "Settings" > "Display & Brightness" > "Auto-Lock."

Software Updates: Keep your smartphone safe by upgrading to the newest iOS version. Enable automatic updates in "Settings" > "General" > "Software Update."

These privacy and security features can help you preserve your personal information and maintain a secure iPhone 15 Pro Max experience.

Accessibility Features

Your iPhone 15 Pro Max comes packed with several accessibility features intended to make the device more usable for those with impairments or others with particular requirements. Here are some significant accessibility features:

VoiceOver: VoiceOver is a screen reader that vocally narrates what's occurring on your screen. It's essential for those with visual impairments. You may activate it in "Settings" > "Accessibility" > "VoiceOver."

Magnifier: The Magnifier function transforms your iPhone into a magnifying glass. It's beneficial for those with poor eyesight. Enable it in "Settings" > "Accessibility" > "Magnifier."

Zoom: Zoom helps you enlarge the whole screen, making the material more apparent. You may enable it under "Settings" > "Accessibility" > "Zoom."

Display & Text Size: Under "Settings" > "Accessibility" > "Display & Text Size," you may alter text size, bold text, and enable more significant accessibility sizes.

Speech: The Speech function reads text out loud. You may change it under "Settings" > "Accessibility" > "Spoken Content."

Voice operation: Voice Control enables users to operate their devices using voice commands. Enable it in "Settings" > "Accessibility" > "Voice Control."

Hearing Features: There are many features for people with hearing problems, including Sound Recognition (alerts for certain noises), Sound Balance, and Hearing Devices settings.

Switch operation: Switch Control lets users operate their device using external switches or buttons. Configure it in "Settings" > "Accessibility" > "Switch Control."

AssistiveTouch: AssistiveTouch offers a configurable on-screen menu that simplifies difficult movements or tasks. Find it under "Settings" > "Accessibility" > "Touch" > "AssistiveTouch."

Guided Access: Guided Access confines your device to a single app and enables you to decide which functions are accessible. You may set it up in "Settings" > "Accessibility" > "Guided Access."

Accessibility Shortcut: Enable an Accessibility Shortcut in "Settings" > "Accessibility" > "Accessibility Shortcut" to rapidly access certain accessibility features by triple-clicking the side or home button.

Text Recognition (OCR): Your device can identify and read text in photos or documents. Use it by snapping a shot and choosing "Recognize Text" in the Photos app.

Subtitles and Captioning: Customize subtitles and caption settings under "Settings" > "Accessibility" > "Subtitles & Captioning."

Speak Screen: To hear the content read out, swipe down from the top of the screen with two fingers.

Braille Support: The iPhone has built-in Braille support and works with various Braille displays.

Color Filters: Adjust display colors for people with color blindness under "Settings" > "Accessibility" > "Display & Text Size" > "Color Filters."

These are just some accessibility features available on your iPhone 15 Pro Max. Apple is dedicated to making its products accessible for all users, and you may explore these options to optimize your iPhone experience depending on your requirements.

VoiceOver and Magnifier

VoiceOver and Magnifier are two vital accessibility capabilities on your iPhone 15 Pro Max, catering to people with vision impairments or those who need magnification. Here's how to utilize them:

VoiceOver: it is a screen reader that reads aloud what's on your iPhone's screen, making it accessible to persons with visual impairments.

Enable VoiceOver:

Open "Settings" on your iPhone.

Go to "Accessibility."

Tap on "VoiceOver."

Toggle the switch to turn on VoiceOver.

Using VoiceOver:

Once activated, VoiceOver will vocally narrate everything on your screen.

To navigate, swipe left or right using one finger to go between items.

Double-tap to choose an item.

Use movements like swipe up or down with two fingers to scroll.

Explore VoiceOver settings in the Accessibility menu for customization possibilities.

VoiceOver Practice: If you're new to VoiceOver, try utilizing the "VoiceOver Practice" option in the VoiceOver settings to become accustomed to gestures and navigation.

Magnifier: The Magnifier converts your iPhone into a strong magnifying glass, ideal for persons with poor eyesight.

Enable Magnifier:

Open "Settings."

Go to "Accessibility."

Tap on "Magnifier."

Toggle the switch to turn on the Magnifier.

Using Magnifier:

To rapidly launch Magnifier, triple-click the side button (or home button if your smartphone has one).

You may set this up in "Settings" > "Accessibility" > "Accessibility Shortcut."

In Magnifier, utilize the slider to change the magnification.

Tap the flashlight symbol to switch on the LED light for enhanced visibility.

Freeze the picture by touching the "Freeze Frame" button.

Use the camera's focusing capability to concentrate on certain details.

Magnifier Filters: The Magnifier also provides several color filters to boost visibility. Swipe left or right to adjust the filter.

Back to Normal: To return to your standard iPhone view, hit the home button (or swipe up from the bottom for smartphones without a home button).

These accessibility capabilities are strong tools that may considerably enhance the usability of your iPhone 15 Pro Max for those with visual impairments or those who require magnification for specific tasks. Experiment with them to discover the settings that work best for you or for the people you're supporting.

Display & Text Size Adjustments

You may alter the display and text size settings on your iPhone 15 Pro Max to make the screen content more pleasant to read and see. Here's how to make these adjustments:

Text Size:

Open Settings: Holding down the Home Screen, choose the "Settings" app.

Display & Text Size: Scroll down and touch "Display & Text Size."

Text Size: Under the "Text Size" area, you'll notice a slider. Slide it to the right to raise the font size or to the left to reduce it.

Preview Text Size: As you move the slider, the sample text below it will change size, providing you a preview of how the text will look.

Bold Text:

Open Settings: Tap the "Settings" app.

Display & Text Size: Go to "Display & Text Size."

Bold Text: Toggle the switch next to "Bold Text" to activate or turn off bold text. Enabling bold text may make content more readable.

Larger Accessibility Sizes:

Open Settings: Access the "Settings" app.

Display & Text Size: Navigate to "Display & Text Size."

Larger Accessibility Sizes: Under the "Text Size" slider, you'll see a "Larger Accessibility Sizes" option. Tap here to explore more fine font size settings.

Alter Text Sizes: You may independently alter different text components, such as "Title Text," "Button Text," and "Label Text," by tapping on them and using the slider that displays.

Accessibility Shortcut: If you wish to easily modify font size using a triple-click of the side button (or home button if your device has one), activate the "Accessibility Shortcut" at the bottom of the page. This enables you to toggle bigger font sizes on and off effortlessly.

Dynamic font: Many applications feature Dynamic Text, which means they modify their font size according to the system settings you've chosen. You may further configure Dynamic Text settings by heading to "Settings" > "Accessibility" > "Display & Text Size" > "Larger Text." Here, you can change the slider for "Larger Accessibility Sizes" for Dynamic Text used in compatible applications.

By altering these settings, you may make your iPhone 15 Pro Max more visually pleasant and accessible, enabling you to read text more readily and have a better overall user experience.

AssistiveTouch

AssistiveTouch is a wonderful accessibility tool on your iPhone 15 Pro Max that generates an on-screen menu with virtual buttons and gestures. It's meant to make using your device simpler for folks with motor skill or dexterity issues. Here's how to utilize AssistiveTouch:

Enabling AssistiveTouch:

Open Settings: From your Home Screen, tap the "Settings" app.

Accessibility: Scroll down and touch on "Accessibility."

Touch: Under the "Touch" section, press "Touch."

AssistiveTouch: Toggle the "AssistiveTouch" switch to make it active. You'll see a virtual button appear on your screen.

Using AssistiveTouch: Once AssistiveTouch is enabled, you may access its functionalities by clicking the virtual button on your screen. Here's how to utilize it:

Tap the Virtual Button: Tap the circular virtual button on your screen to activate the AssistiveTouch menu.

Custom Actions: The menu provides numerous choices and actions you may configure, such as "Home," "Control Center," "Notification Center," "Device," "Gestures," and "Favorites."

Home Button Replacement: If your physical Home Button is not functioning or you choose not to use it, you may utilize AssistiveTouch's "Home" action as a virtual Home Button.

Unique Gestures: Under "Gestures," you may build unique gestures for various activities. This is beneficial if you have problems using typical touchscreen motions.

Custom Actions: You may add your favorite actions to the AssistiveTouch menu for easy access. Just touch "Customize Top Level Menu" to add or rearrange activities.

Device: The "Device" section includes choices to change volume, lock the screen, take a screenshot, and rotate the screen.

Favorites: The "Favorites" area enables you to store certain gestures or actions as favorites for convenient access.

Moving the Button: You may relocate the AssistiveTouch virtual button by touching and dragging it to your chosen spot on the screen.

Customization and Preferences: To customize AssistiveTouch further, go to "Settings" > "Accessibility" > "Touch" > "AssistiveTouch." Here, you can adjust settings such as the idle opacity (how transparent the button becomes when not in use), enable "Always Show Menu," and configure "Double-Tap" and "Long Press" actions for the virtual button.

AssistiveTouch is a flexible feature that may dramatically enhance the usability of your iPhone 15 Pro Max for users with motor or dexterity issues. Still, it can be handy for anybody who needs rapid access to basic operations. Experiment with its options to adapt it to your unique requirements and interests.

Managing Battery Life

Preserving battery life ensures your iPhone 15 Pro Max remains charged throughout the day. Here are some suggestions and tactics to manage and maximize your device's battery life:

Check Battery Usage: Go to "Settings" > "Battery" to obtain a breakdown of which applications and services are using the most battery power. This might help you identify energy-hungry applications.

Enable Low Power Mode: Activate Low Power Mode when your battery is going low or you want to prolong battery life. You may activate it in "Settings" > "Battery" > "Low Power Mode."

Adjust Screen Brightness: Lower your screen brightness or activate Auto-Brightness in "Settings" > "Display & Brightness."

Consume Dark Mode: If your iPhone has an OLED screen, utilizing Dark Mode may conserve battery by showing more black pixels, which consume less power.

Manage Background App Refresh: Disable Background App Refresh for applications you don't need to update in the background. Configure this under "Settings" > "General" > "Background App Refresh."

Wi-Fi and Cellular: Turn off Wi-Fi and cellular data when you're not using them. Use Airplane Mode in poor signal locations.

Location Services: Review and restrict app access to your location under "Settings" > "Privacy" > "Location Services."

Push Email: Set your email accounts to retrieve fresh emails manually or at longer intervals instead of utilizing Push. You may alter this under "Settings" > "Mail" > "Accounts" > "Fetch New Data."

App Updates: Keep your applications updated to guarantee they employ the newest energy-efficient technology.

Widgets: Remove unneeded widgets from your Today View by swiping right on your Home Screen and clicking "Edit."

Push Notifications: Reduce the amount of applications that give you push notifications. Go to "Settings" > "Notifications" and change notification settings for each app.

Auto-Lock: Set your device to lock after a shorter time of inactivity automatically. Adjust this under "Settings" > "Display & Brightness" > "Auto-Lock."

App Background Activity: Close unnecessary applications running in the background by double-clicking the Home Button (or swiping up from the bottom on devices without a Home Button) and sliding away apps from the app switcher.

Battery Health: Check your battery's health under "Settings" > "Battery" > "Battery Health." If your battery health is drastically compromised, consider replacing it at an Apple Store.

Avoid Extreme conditions: Extremely hot or cold conditions might impact battery performance. Keep your gadget within the recommended temperature range.

Use Optimized Battery Charging: Turn on Optimized Battery Charging in "Settings" > "Battery" > "Battery Health." This helps slow down battery aging.

Background App Activity: In "Settings" > "Privacy" > "following," you may restrict applications from following your activity across other apps and websites, which can also help preserve battery life.

Implementing these methods may help you control and optimize the battery life of your iPhone 15 Pro Max, ensuring it lasts longer between charges and operates effectively.

Battery Usage Tips and Optimizing Battery Health

Preserving your iPhone 15 Pro Max's battery life and improving battery health are vital for long-term performance. Here are some strategies to control energy consumption and maintain optimum battery health:

Battery Usage Tips:

Enable Low Power Mode: When your battery is running low, enable Low Power Mode under "Settings" > "Battery" > "Low Power Mode." It limits background operations to increase battery life.

Screen Brightness: Lower your screen brightness or activate Auto-Brightness in "Settings" > "Display & Brightness."

Dark Mode: If your iPhone has an OLED screen, utilizing Dark Mode helps conserve power by showing more black pixels.

Background App Refresh: For any applications that don't require background updates, turn off Background App Refresh. Configure this under "Settings" > "General" > "Background App Refresh."

Wi-Fi and Cellular Data: Turn down Wi-Fi and cellular data when not used, particularly in poor signal regions. Use Airplane Mode to deactivate all wireless connections as required.

Location Services: Review and restrict app access to your location in "Settings" > "Privacy" > "Location Services." Use the "While Using the App" option wherever feasible.

Push Email: Set your email accounts to retrieve fresh emails manually or at longer intervals instead of utilizing Push. Configure this under "Settings" > "Mail" > "Accounts" > "Fetch New Data."

App Updates: Keep your applications updated to guarantee they employ the newest energy-efficient technology.

Widgets: Remove unneeded widgets from your Today View by swiping right on your Home Screen and clicking "Edit."

Push Notifications: Reduce the amount of applications that give you push notifications. Customize notification settings for each app in "Settings" > "Notifications."

Auto-Lock: Set your device to lock after a shorter time of inactivity automatically. Adjust this under "Settings" > "Display & Brightness" > "Auto-Lock."

Optimizing Battery Health:

Battery Health: Check your battery's health under "Settings" > "Battery" > "Battery Health." If the Maximum Capacity is considerably reduced (usually below 80%), consider having the battery changed at an Apple Store.

Optimized Battery Charging: Enable this function in "Settings" > "Battery" > "Battery Health." It helps slow down battery aging by learning regular charging patterns and decreasing peak battery demand.

Avoid Extreme Temperatures: Temperature extremes might affect how well a battery performs. Keep your device within the specified temperature range (0°C to 35°C or 32°F to 95°F).

Regular Charging: It's normally preferable to keep your battery charged between 20% and 80% for day-to-day usage. Avoid letting it deplete fully before setting.

Charge with Quality Accessories: Use Apple-certified chargers and cords to guarantee safe and efficient charging.

Unplug at 100%: Avoid leaving your gadget plugged in at 100% for lengthy durations. Unplug it after it's ultimately charged.

Software upgrades: Keep your iOS version up-to-date since Apple typically offers enhancements for battery life in promotions.

Implementing these steps can help you minimize energy consumption and lengthen the overall longevity of your iPhone 15 Pro Max's battery, ensuring it stays in excellent health for a prolonged period.

iCloud and Data Backup

iCloud is Apple's cloud storage and backup service that lets you securely store your data, keep it up-to-date across your devices, and ensure a backup in case of data loss. Here's how to utilize iCloud and back up your data on your iPhone 15 Pro Max:

Setting Up iCloud: When you initially set up your iPhone, you'll be requested to log in with your Apple ID or create one. Your Apple ID will be connected to your iCloud account.

iCloud Backup: The Cloud can automatically backup the data on your iPhone, including photographs, movies, app data, settings, and more. To activate iCloud Backup:

Go to "Settings."

Tap your Apple ID at the top.

Tap "iCloud."

Scroll down and hit "iCloud Backup."

Toggle on "iCloud Backup."

Tap "Back Up Now" to begin an instant backup.

iCloud backups occur automatically while your smartphone is connected to Wi-Fi, charging, and locked. You may check the last backup time on the same "iCloud Backup" screen.

Manage iCloud Storage: iCloud gives 5 GB of free storage, but you may need additional space for backups and files. To manage your iCloud storage:

Go to "Settings."

Tap your Apple ID at the top.

Tap "iCloud."

Tap "Manage Storage."

Here, you may check how your storage is utilized, remove backups, and upgrade to a bigger storage plan if required.

iCloud Drive: iCloud Drive enables you to save files and documents in the cloud, making them available across your Apple devices. You may access iCloud Drive via the Files app on your iPhone.

Photographs in iCloud: iCloud Photos automatically uploads and saves your photographs and videos in iCloud. To enable it:

Go to "Settings."

Tap your Apple ID.

Tap "iCloud."

Tap "Photos."

Toggle on "iCloud Photos."

With iCloud Photos, your material is available across all your Apple devices, and changes you make, such as edits or deletions, sync smoothly.

Find My: Find My iPhone helps you to find your cellphone if it's lost or stolen. Make sure it's activated under "Settings" > [your name] > "Find My" > "Find My iPhone."

iCloud Keychain: iCloud Keychain securely keeps your passwords and credit card details, making them accessible on all your Apple devices. You may activate it under "Settings" > [your name] > "iCloud" > "Keychain."

By utilizing iCloud and conducting frequent backups, you can guarantee your data is secure and accessible, even if you lose your iPhone or move to a new one. It's a key aspect of preserving your device and its data.

iCloud Backup and Data Recovery

iCloud Backup is an easy solution to preserve your iPhone's data and settings. If you ever need to restore data from an iCloud Backup, or if you're setting up a new iPhone, here's how to do it:

Creating an iCloud Backup: Before you can restore data from an iCloud Backup, you must have previously generated a backup. To develop an iCloud Backup:

Connect to Wi-Fi: Ensure your iPhone is linked to a Wi-Fi network.

Plug into Power: Connect your gadget to a charger or check it has adequate battery life.

Enable iCloud Backup:

Go to "Settings."

Tap your Apple ID at the top.

Tap "iCloud."

Scroll down and hit "iCloud Backup."

Toggle on "iCloud Backup."

Tap "Back Up Now" to begin an instant backup.

Automatic Backups: iCloud will automatically back up your smartphone daily while connected to Wi-Fi, charging, and locked.

Recovering Data from iCloud Backup: When setting up a new iPhone or restoring your existing one from an iCloud Backup:

Initial Setup: Turn on your new iPhone or reset your existing one (if you're starting fresh). Until you see the "Apps & Data" screen, follow the instructions on the screen.

Choose "Restore from iCloud Backup": Select "Restore from iCloud Backup" on the "Apps & Data" screen.

Sign In to iCloud: Enter your Apple ID and password.

Select a Backup: From the available backups, select the iCloud backup you want to restore. Select the most current one that has the data you require.

Stay Connected: Keep your device connected to Wi-Fi and power throughout the repair process. The time it takes depends on the backup size and internet connection speed.

Finish Setup: Once the restoration is complete, follow the remaining on-screen prompts to finish the setup. After the procedure, your iPhone should be restored to the condition it was in when the selected iCloud Backup was made. This includes your applications, photographs, settings, and more.

Important Notes: You may also pick which data categories to recover during setup, such as Photos, Contacts, Messages, and more. Suppose you're not setting up a new iPhone and must retrieve particular data. In that case, you may selectively restore data from an iCloud Backup using options like "Reset All Settings" as well as "Erase All Content and Settings" under the "Settings" application. However, be careful since this will wipe your present device data. Using iCloud Backup and data recovery is an easy method to guarantee your data stays secure and accessible, even if you switch to a new device or face unexpected data loss.

Troubleshooting and FAQs

Battery Drain Issues:

Issue: Rapid battery depletion.

Solution:

Check Battery Usage in "Settings" > "Battery" to detect power-hungry programs.

Enable Low Power Mode.

Adjust screen brightness and utilize Dark Mode.

Update to the newest iOS version.

Consider battery health if your device's battery deteriorates.

App Crashes or Freezing:

Issue: Apps crash or freeze.

Solution:

Restart your iPhone.

Update the malfunctioning app.

Delete and reinstall the app.

Check for iOS updates.

If it continues, contact the app's creator or Apple Support.

Slow Performance:

Issue: Slow overall device performance.

Solution:

Close background applications.

Clear storage space by uninstalling useless programs or media.

Reset device settings (Settings > General > Reset > Reset All Settings).

Restore the device from a backup if required.

Wi-Fi or Cellular Issues:

Issue: Wi-Fi or cellular connection difficulties.

Solution:

Toggle Wi-Fi or cellular data off and on.

iPhone 15 Pro Max Phone Guide

Restart your router or modem.

Reset network settings (Settings > General > Reset > Reset Network Settings).

Contact your service provider for help.

Storage Full:

Issue: Running out of storage capacity.

Solution:

Delete unneeded applications, photographs, and videos.

Use iCloud or other cloud storage for photographs and documents.

Offload applications under "Settings" > "General" > "iPhone Storage."

Forgotten Passcode:

Issue: Forgot your device passcode.

Solution:

If you've set up Face ID or Touch ID, use it for authentication.

Restore your device using iTunes or Finder on a PC.

Lost or Stolen Device:

Issue: Lost or stolen iPhone.

Solution:

Use Find My iPhone to locate, lock, or wipe your smartphone remotely.

Report the loss to local law police and your cellphone provider.

No Sound or Audio Issues:

Issue: No sound during calls or media playback.

Solution:

Check the device's volume settings.

Ensure your gadget isn't in quiet mode (check the mute switch).

Inspect the speaker grille for debris.

Restart your device.

iCloud Backup Issues:

Issue: iCloud Backup won't function.

Solution:

Ensure you're connected to Wi-Fi.

Verify that iCloud storage isn't full.

Check iCloud settings for backup limits.

Sign out and back into your iCloud account.

Touchscreen Problems:

Issue: Unresponsive touchscreen or touch input difficulties.

Solution:

Clean the screen and remove any screen protector.

Restart your device.

Update to the newest iOS version.

If hardware-related, contact Apple Support.

Suppose you need help with any particular difficulties addressed here. In that case, you can always visit the official Apple Support website, call Apple Support directly, or, for assistance in person, stop by an Apple Store. Apple's support resources are broad and may help you fix various issues with your iPhone 15 Pro Max.

Common Issues with Solutions and Frequently Asked Questions

App Crashes or Freezing:

Issue: Apps crash or freeze.

Solution:

Restart your iPhone.

Update the malfunctioning app.

Delete and reinstall the app.

Check for iOS updates.

If it continues, contact the app's creator or Apple Support.

Slow Performance:

Issue: Slow overall device performance.

Solution:

Close background applications.

Clear storage space by uninstalling useless programs or media.

Reset device settings (Settings > General > Reset > Reset All Settings).

Restore the device from a backup if required.

Battery Drain Issues:

Issue: Rapid battery depletion.

Solution:

Check Battery Usage in "Settings" > "Battery" to detect power-hungry programs.

Enable Low Power Mode.

Adjust screen brightness and utilize Dark Mode.

Update to the newest iOS version.

Consider battery health if your device's battery deteriorates.

Wi-Fi or Cellular Issues:

Issue: Wi-Fi or cellular connection difficulties.

Solution:

Toggle Wi-Fi or cellular data off and on.

Restart your router or modem.

Reset network settings (Settings > General > Reset > Reset Network Settings).

Contact your service provider for help.

Storage Full:
Issue: Running out of storage capacity.
Solution:

Delete unneeded applications, photographs, and videos.

Use iCloud or other cloud storage for photographs and documents.

Offload applications under "Settings" > "General" > "iPhone Storage."

Forgotten Passcode:
Issue: Forgot your device passcode.
Solution:
If you've set up Face ID or Touch ID, use it for authentication.

Restore your device using iTunes or Finder on a PC.

Lost or Stolen Device:

Issue: Lost or stolen iPhone.

Solution:

Use Find My iPhone to locate, lock, or wipe your smartphone remotely.

Report the loss to local law police and your cellphone provider.

No Sound or Audio Issues:

Issue: No sound during calls or media playback.

Solution:

Check the device's volume settings.

Ensure your gadget isn't in quiet mode (check the mute switch).

Inspect the speaker grille for debris.

Restart your device.

iCloud Backup Issues:

Issue: iCloud Backup won't function.

Solution:

Ensure you're connected to Wi-Fi.

Verify that iCloud storage isn't full.

Check iCloud settings for backup limits.

Sign out and back into your iCloud account.

Touchscreen Problems:

Issue: Unresponsive touchscreen or touch input difficulties.

Solution:

Clean the screen and remove any screen protector.

Restart your device.

Update to the newest iOS version.

If hardware-related, contact Apple Support.

Frequently Asked Questions (FAQs):

How can I capture a screenshot on my iPhone 15 Pro Max?

-Press the Volume Up and Side (or Power) buttons simultaneously.

How can I check my battery health?

-Go to "Settings" > "Battery" > "Battery Health" to check your battery's maximum capacity and peak performance potential.

Can I use Face ID with a mask?

-In iOS 15.4 and later, you can set up Face ID to function with a mask by navigating to "Settings" > "Face ID & Passcode" > "Unlock with Face ID."

How do I upgrade my iPhone's software?

-Go to "Settings" > "General" > "Software Update" to check for and install the newest iOS upgrades.

Please note that software features and solutions may change with iOS upgrades, so it's a good habit to keep your iPhone's software up-to-date to enjoy the newest features and enhancements.

Tips and Tricks

Customizing the Control Center: You may personalize the Control Center by navigating to "Settings" > "Control Center." Add or delete shortcuts and widgets to adapt it to your requirements.

Quick Access to Camera: Swipe left on the lock screen or touch and hold the Camera app icon to quickly access the camera, even while your smartphone is locked.

Dark Mode: Enable Dark Mode in "Settings" > "Display & Brightness" to decrease eye strain and conserve battery life on OLED panels.

Rear Tap: Under "Accessibility" > "Touch," you may activate "Back Tap" to conduct activities by touching the rear of your phone. Customize it for things like capturing screenshots or activating applications.

Text Selection: To swiftly choose text, touch the space bar on the keyboard and slide your finger to move the cursor. Or, double-tap a word to pick it and triple-tap to choose a phrase.

Face ID alternate look: Face ID may have a different appearance set up by going to "Settings" > "Face ID & Passcode" > "Set Up an Alternate Appearance."

Live text: iOS 15 introduces Live Text, which enables you to interact with text in photographs. Touch on text in photographs to copy, check-up, or translate.

Focus Mode: Use Focus Mode to filter alerts and tailor what goes through when you need to focus. Configure it in "Settings" > "Focus."

Quick Path Keyboard: Slide your finger over the keyboard to text without lifting it. It's a quicker method to type text.

Siri Shortcuts: Create Siri Shortcuts to automate tasks. Go to "Settings" > "Siri & Search" > "Siri Shortcuts" to set up your shortcuts.

Privacy Report: In Safari, hit the "AA" symbol in the address bar and pick "Privacy Report" to examine how websites monitor your surfing activities.

Hide My Email: When signing up for services, utilize "Hide My Email" to generate temporary email accounts forwarded to your principal inbox. Find this functionality in "Settings" > "Mail" > "Hide My Email."

Two-Factor Authentication: Enhance security by setting Two-Factor Authentication for your Apple ID. Go to "Settings" > [your name] > "Password & Security."

Emergency SOS: Quickly summon emergency services by pushing and holding the Side (or Power) button and either Volume button.

Backing Up to iCloud: Enable iCloud Backup in "Settings" > [your name] > "iCloud" > "iCloud Backup" to automatically back up your smartphone.

Scan Documents: Use the Notes app to scan and store documents. Create a new note, hit the camera icon, and choose "Scan Documents."

Share Your Location: Use the Messages app to let friends and family know where you are in real time. Tap their name in a conversation, pick "Info," and then "Share My Location."

Offload Unused Apps: Save space by activating "Offload Unused Apps" under "Settings" > "General" > "iPhone Storage."

App Library: Swipe left on your final home screen page to reach the App Library, which organizes your applications into categories.

Quick access to options: Use the Search bar in the Settings app to quickly access certain options without browsing through menus.

These tips and techniques should help you manage and operate your iPhone 15 Pro Max more effectively, making your everyday activities simpler and more fun.

Hidden Features and Shortcuts

Quickly Access Magnifier: Triple-click the Side (or Power) button to activate the Magnifier, which may help you zoom in on text or objects.

Instantly Redial the Last Number: To rapidly redial the last number you called, just hit the green Call icon in the Phone app.

One-Handed Keyboard: You may activate a one-handed keyboard for easier typing on bigger displays. Press and hold the emoji or globe symbol on the keyboard, then pick the left or right one-handed keyboard.

Safari Tab Groups: In Safari, you can create Tab Groups to arrange your open tabs. Tap the Tabs icon, then scroll down and click "New Tab Group" to get started.

Audio Sharing with AirPods: If you and a buddy have AirPods, you can share audio from your iPhone. Connect both sets of AirPods, go to the Control Center, hit the audio playback widget, and pick "Share Audio."

Keyboard Trackpad Mode: Turn your iPhone's keyboard into a trackpad for accurate cursor positioning. On the keyboard, press and hold the Spacebar, and the keys will become blank. Now, you may slide your finger to move the cursor.

Measure App: Use the Measure app to measure things or places by pointing your iPhone at them. It's a great tool for rapid measurements.

Private Browsing: In Safari, touch and hold the "+" button to launch a new tab in Private Browsing mode. This stops your browsing history from being kept.

QR Code Scanning: Your iPhone's camera can read QR codes without having separate software. Just open the Camera app and aim it at the QR code.

Undo Typing: Shake your iPhone to undo typing. A pop-up will display, enabling you to undo or redo your input.

Conceal Notification Previews: You may conceal notification previews on the lock screen for increased privacy. Go to "Settings" > "Notifications" > "Show Previews" and pick "When Unlocked."

Swipe to Go Back: In many applications, you may swipe from the left side of the screen to go back to the previous screen or page.

Silent Unknown Callers: To mute calls from unknown numbers, activate "mute Unknown Callers" in "Settings" > "Phone." Calls from your contacts will still ring through.

Focus Mode Automation: Set up Focus modes to activate automatically depending on your location, the time of day, or current activity. Customize this under "Settings" > "Focus."

Smart Data Mode: Smart Data Mode under "Settings" > "Cellular" will automatically transition between 5G and LTE to preserve battery life when high-speed data isn't required.

Sleep Timer: In the Clock app, establish a sleep timer for your music or podcast. Play music, then open the Clock app, hit "Timer," and pick "Stop Playing."

Customize Vibrations: Create bespoke vibration patterns for specific contacts or alerts under "Settings" > "Sounds & Haptics" > "Ringtone" > "Vibration."

Secret Emojis: There are secret emoji characters that you may access. For example, hold down the "Like" button in the Messages app to get a secret heart emoji effect.

These secret features and shortcuts may make your iPhone 15 Pro Max more flexible and user-friendly. Explore them to improve your smartphone experience.

Enhancing Productivity

Use Widgets: Customize your home screen with widgets to rapidly access critical information and execute actions without launching applications. To add widgets, press and hold on the home screen, hit the "+" button in the upper left, and pick from the available widgets.

Create Shortcuts: The Shortcuts software enables you to automate processes and create unique shortcuts. For example, you may build a shortcut to send a specified message to a contact or set up a shortcut to start a certain playlist when you attach your headphones.

Set Up Focus Mode: Use Focus Mode to limit distractions and remain productive. Customize Focus modes for work, personal leisure, or specialized hobbies. It filters alerts and lets only critical ones through.

Use Reminders and Notes: The Reminders and Notes applications may help you keep organized. Create to-do lists, establish deadlines, and write down ideas. You may also use Siri to add stuff to your reminders or notes.

Calendar Integration: Sync your calendar with your iPhone and set up event alerts. You may also utilize natural language processing to build events rapidly. For example, say, "Create a meeting with John at 2 PM tomorrow."

Multitasking with Split View: On bigger iPhone models, utilize Split View incompatible applications to work on two tasks concurrently. Swipe down from the top of the screen in a compatible app to enable Split View.

Keyboard Shortcuts: Take use of keyboard shortcuts while typing. For example, touch and hold particular keys to access special characters or shortcuts for copy, cut, paste, and undo.

Scan Documents: The Notes app contains a built-in document scanner. Use it to scan and save tangible documents as PDFs. This is important for maintaining records and becoming paperless.

Use Siri for Hands-Free chores: Siri can assist you with various chores, from setting timers and sending messages to accessing information on the web. Activate Siri with a voice command or push and hold the Side (or Power) button.

iCloud Syncing: Ensure your essential papers and data are synchronized with iCloud so that you can access them from any Apple device. This keeps your work up-to-date across all platforms.

Keyboard Dictation: Use the built-in dictation capability on the keyboard for hands-free typing. To speak your words, tap the keyboard's microphone icon.

Use Third-Party Productivity applications: Explore the App Store for productivity applications that may assist you with certain chores. Whether project management, note-taking, or document editing, applications are customized to your requirements.

Offline Access: Download critical papers, emails, or files for offline access when you know you'll be without a steady internet connection.

Accessibility tools: Explore accessibility tools like VoiceOver, Magnifier, and AssistiveTouch to suit varied demands and make your device more user-friendly.

Screen Time: Monitor your screen time and app use under "Settings" > "Screen Time." Set app restrictions to minimize overuse and measure your progress in remaining productive.

By implementing these techniques and leveraging the built-in capabilities of your iPhone 15 Pro Max, you can simplify your workflow, remain organized, and enhance your overall productivity.

Warranty and Support

Warranty and support for your iPhone 15 Pro Max are vital for ensuring your device performs correctly and is protected in case of complications. Here's everything you need to know:

Guarantee: When you buy a new iPhone, it normally comes with a limited one-year guarantee from Apple. This warranty covers manufacturing faults and hardware problems that may emerge during regular usage.

AppleCare+ for iPhone: Apple provides an extended warranty and support package called AppleCare+. This plan extends your coverage to two years from the original purchase date and includes up to two incidences of accidental damage coverage (subject to a service charge). AppleCare+ also gives priority access to Apple support, which may be beneficial for troubleshooting and technical assistance.

Checking Warranty Status: You can check the warranty status of your iPhone by visiting the Apple website and entering your device's serial number or by calling Apple Support.

Support Options:

Apple gives different support options:

Apple Support App: Download the Apple Support app from the App Store to read articles and videos and contact Apple Support

Online Support: Visit the Apple Support website for troubleshooting tips, manuals, and support tools

Apple Store: If there's an Apple Store close by, arrange an appointment at the Genius Bar for in-person help.

Phone Support: Call Apple Support for phone assistance. The number varies by area.

Repair Services: If your iPhone requires repair, Apple provides numerous options:

Ship-in Service: You may ship your iPhone to Apple for repair.

Apple Authorized Servicing Provider: Locate an authorized repair provider in your region for in-person servicing.

Apple Store: Visit an Apple Store for in-person repair services or assistance.

Software Support: Apple constantly releases iOS upgrades that offer new features, security patches, and bug fixes. Your iPhone should get software upgrades for many years after its debut.

Backup Your Data: Before seeking repair or assistance, it's a recommended habit to back up your iPhone's data to iCloud or your computer to avoid data loss during the service process.

AppleCare+ Renewal: You have the option to renew your AppleCare+ coverage for extra years. Consider this if you want to retain your iPhone for a lengthy term.

Remember that warranty coverage and support options might vary by location and may be subject to change over time. It's suggested to check the official Apple website or contact Apple Support for the most up-to-date information on your iPhone 15 Pro Max's warranty and accessible support options.

Warranty Information

Please note that warranty policies and conditions may change over time, so it's crucial to check the current terms on the official Apple website or contact Apple Support for the most up-to-date information. Typically, Apple provides the following:

Limited guarantee: When you acquire a new iPhone, it normally comes with a limited one-year guarantee from Apple. This warranty covers manufacturing faults and hardware problems that may develop during regular operation. It does not cover unintentional damage.

AppleCare+: AppleCare+ is an optional extended warranty and support package Apple provides. It extends the coverage for your iPhone to two years from the original purchase date. AppleCare+ offers technical help and up to two incidences of accidental damage coverage (subject to a service cost). You may buy AppleCare+ for your iPhone either at the time of purchase or within 60 days of your iPhone purchase.

Checking Warranty Status: You may check the warranty status of your iPhone by visiting the Apple website and entering your device's serial number or by calling Apple Support.

Apple's guarantee Coverage: Apple's guarantee covers hardware components and manufacturing defects, including faults with the device's display, battery, camera, and other built-in components. The damage resulting from accidents, unauthorized repairs, alterations made by third parties, and issues brought on by software updates are not covered under the guarantee.

Repair Services: If your iPhone needs repair or service, you may contact Apple Support, visit an Apple Store, or find an Apple Authorized Service Provider in your region for help. Repairs may be covered under warranty, AppleCare+, or subject to out-of-warranty costs, depending on the exact problem and your device's warranty status.

It's essential to read and understand the terms and restrictions of your warranty coverage, particularly if you're contemplating getting AppleCare+ or having any difficulties with your iPhone. Remember that the warranty terms and coverage might change by location, so it's important to check the latest specifics on the official Apple website or call Apple Support directly.

Contacting Apple Support

You may contact Apple Support via several means, depending on your taste and region. Here are some typical methods to get in contact with Apple Support:

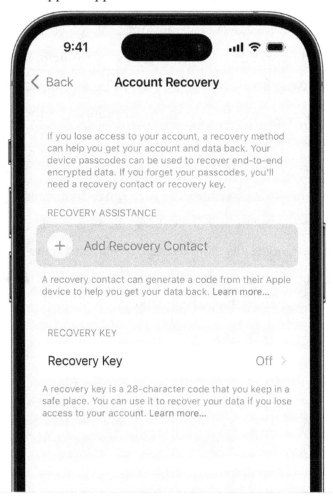

Apple Support Website: Visit the official Apple Support website at support.apple.com. Here, you may discover useful articles, tutorials, and troubleshooting tools for your iPhone and other Apple devices. Many common difficulties may be fixed by following the step-by-step directions offered.

Apple Support App: If you have an iPhone, go to the App Store and download the "Apple Support" app. This app offers a handy method to access help materials and connect with Apple help specialists.

Phone Support: To connect directly with an Apple Support specialist, you may phone Apple's customer support number. The phone number may change based on your area. You can locate the relevant phone number for your location on the Apple Support page.

Online Chat: Some locations provide online chat help via the Apple help website or the Apple Support app. You may speak with a support professional in real time to obtain help with your concerns or difficulties.

Twitter help: Apple also offers help via its official Twitter account, @AppleSupport. You may send them a tweet or direct message with any questions or concerns.

Apple Store Appointments: If you're suffering hardware-related difficulties with your iPhone, you may arrange an appointment at an Apple Store's Genius Bar. Apple Store personnel can diagnose and suggest solutions for your device.

Email Support: In certain situations, you may be able to email Apple Support via the Apple Support website. Response times may vary.

When calling Apple Support, it's important to have your iPhone's serial number and warranty information handy, particularly if you're seeking assistance with a specific device. This information may accelerate the support process and guarantee your queries are answered efficiently.

Conclusion and Final Remarks

In conclusion, the iPhone 15 Pro Max is a strong and flexible gadget that can boost your work, keep you connected, and offer enjoyment. With its sophisticated features, amazing photography capabilities, and the newest iOS upgrades, it's intended to fulfill various demands.

Remember to explore the numerous features and activities covered in this book, from fundamental operations like making calls and sending messages to sophisticated ones such as managing images and utilizing productivity tools. Regularly upgrading your device's software and using Apple's support and warranty services will help guarantee a seamless and pleasurable experience.

If you ever have concerns or face troubles with your iPhone, don't hesitate to contact Apple Support for assistance. They're available to help you get the most out of your equipment and handle any problems.

www.ingramcontent.com/pod-product-compliance
Lightning Source LLC
LaVergne TN
LVHW051655050326
832903LV00032B/3818